AUSSIE SLANG DOWN UNDER

Pictorial Press Australia

This edition published by Pictorial Press Australia
PO Box 388 Corinda Brisbane Qld 4075 Australia
Ph 07 3716 01 04 Fax 07 3716 01 05
robert@pictorialpress.com.au

Reprinted 2012
Reprinted 2013
Reprinted 2014
Reprinted 2016

ISBN 978 1 876561 09 3

Compiling by Robert Brown, Sue Tester, Selena Webber

Produced by Jade Productions

**AUSSIE
SLANG
DOWN UNDER**

Australian slang utilises humour, wit, rhymes, bizarre experiences from the bush to the beach, familiar and personal to portray how experiences shape language and identity. For example, *'have a burl'* at something is similar to *'have a crack'*, and both phrases reflect a history of Australian improvisation and hard work as part of working in the bush.

Please note that some of the words and expressions in **Aussie Slang Down Under** may cause offence. It is not recommended to use such words and expressions, but they have been included as **Aussie Slang Down Under** is a book about the use of language whether it be good or bad.

A1   first class
ABC   Australian Broadcasting Corporation or Aunty
AC DC   bisexual
AFL   Australian football league
AO   adults only
APC   hand-wash arm pits and crotch
A big deal   important, serious
A bit much   rude, excessive
A bit rich   over-priced
A okay   very good
A over t/Arse over tit   falling over, stumbling
A real shit   a horrible person
Above board   legal
Abso-bloody-lutely   positively yes
Ace   the best, very good
Act the goat   foolish behaviour
Adams ale   water
Aerial ping pong   Australian Rules Football
Aggro   aggressive behaviour
Aggy pipe   terracotta drainage pipe
Akubra   a wide-brimmed hat
Al Capone   telephone
Alice, the   Alice Springs
Alko   an alcoholic, heavy drinker
All ears   listening attentively
All piss and wind   insincere, boastful
All rounder   good at many tasks or sports
All smiles   happy
All systems go   ready
Alrighty   okay, yes

Akubra is a popular brand of **Aussie** fur felt hats. The wide brim is a typical part of **Ozzie** culture.

Always in the shit always in trouble
Always on the go always busy
Amber fluid beer
Ambo ambulance
Ammo ammunition
Amp 1. amplifier; 2. get excited
Anal 1. fussy, perfectionist, neat; 2. obsessive
Ankle biter infant or young child
ANZAC Australian and New Zealand Army Corps
Anchors car brakes
Ant's pants very good
Ape shit raving mad
Apple Isle Tasmania
Apples, she'll be it'll be all right
Argue the toss disagree
Argy bargy an argument
Around the bend crazy, mad
Arse end worst part, tail end
Arse into gear get going, moving, start
Arse off depart
Arsey very lucky
Arthur or Martha a state of confusion
Arvo afternoon
As crook as a dog very unwell
As if expression of complete disagreement, disbelief
As pissed as a newt very drunk
As rough as guts 1. poor workmanship, rough; 2. uncouth person
As the crow flies travel in a direct line
At death's door dying, seriously ill
At full tilt at full speed

ANZAC Day, 25th April is an important national occasion. It marks the anniversary of the first major military action fought by Australian and New Zealand forces in the Battle of Gallipoli during the First World War. The soldiers became known as **ANZACs**.

At odds   disagreement
At the crack of dawn   daybreak
At the drop of a hat   immediately
At the wheel   in control, in charge
Atta boy   approval
Aussie/Ozzie   an Australian person
Aussie battler   a working class person
Aussie rules   Australian football
Aussie salute   brushing away flies with your hand
'Ave a go   do something, get started
Avos   avocados
Awesome   1. excellent; 2. high quality
Axe/Axed   dismissed, get the sack
BBQ   barbeque
BYO   1. bring your own alcohol; 2. unlicensed restaurant
Back down   retreat from an argument
Back of beyond   a remote area
Back of Bourke   remote outback area
Backhander   hit with the back of the hand
Bad mouth   criticise unfavourably
Bad trot   period of misfortunes and bad luck
Bag   1. claim first; 2. unattractive woman
Bag of fruit   a suit
Bail out   to depart, leave a situation
Bail up   to physically corner somebody
Ball and chain   wife
Balmain bug   crab or crustacean
Banana bender   a Queenslander
Banged up   pregnant
Banjo   1. frying pan; 2. a shovel

Barbie barbeque
Banker a river or stream in flood
Barney an argument or fight
Barra fish called a Barramundi
Barrack to cheer on a sporting team
Bash 1. attempt; 2. party; 3. assault someone
Batch living on one's own
Bathers swimming costume
Battler one who struggles in life
Beanie knitted brimless cap
Beaut/beauty fantastic, excellent
Bee's knees great, fantastic
Beer belly beer drinking paunch
Belly-ache to complain
Belly-button navel
Bellyful too much of anything
Belt 1. move quickly; 2. hit
Bender drinking binge
Bend the elbow a heavy drinker
Betcha I bet you
Better half wife
Bevan lout, hooligan
Bewdie 1. beautiful, good; 2. approval
Bible basher a religious person
Biddie old woman
Bikkie biscuit
Big girl's blouse 1. effeminate male; 2. timid
Big red male red kangaroo
Big smoke a big city, usually a capital city
Big spit vomit

Rock on over for a **barbie** Saturday **arvo**. There'll be **heaps** of **snags**, **prawns** and **chook**. **BYO**, down a **few coldies** and **veg out**.

Big-note oneself   to boast or brag about oneself

Billabong   a waterhole

Billycan (billy)   a metal container to brew tea over the campfire

Billycart   homemade cart steered by ropes

Bin   garbage can

Bindi   plant with prickly seeds

Bingle   a minor car crash

Birthday suit   naked

Bite ya bum   be quiet, shut up

Bitser   an animal or person of mixed blood

Bizzo   doing business

Black stump, beyond the   long distance away

Blind   very drunk person

Blind Freddie   an unperceptive person

Blob   1. a fat person; 2. cricket score; out with no runs

Blockie   drive around the block

Bloke   a male person, fellow, chap

Blood house   a disorderly public house with a reputation for violence

Blood nut   a person with red hair

Bloody   very (the great Australian adjective)

Bloody galah   a silly person

Bloody oath!   I agree

Blotto   very drunk person

Blow   1. have a rest; 2. fail in something

Blow in   an uninvited person, stranger

Blow in the bag   breathalyser test

Blow me down   expression of surprise

Blower   a telephone

Blowie   a blowfly

Bludge   impose on one's generosity

Blowies are large, metallic coloured flies that lay their eggs on carcasses and other organic matter.

9

Bludger   a very lazy person

Blue   a fight

Blue-arsed fly   a blue blowfly

Blue heeler   an Australian cattle dog

Blue, make a   make a mistake

Bluey   1. swag; 2. traffic ticket; 3. redhead

Bluey   4. blue cattle dog; 5. bluebottle jellyfish

Blue flyer   female red kangaroo

Blunder   a mistake

Boardies   board shorts

Bobby dazzler   something very good

Bob's your uncle   all is well

Bodgy   false, worthless

Bog   going to the toilet

Bog house   outside toilet

Bog in   eat heartily

Bogan   loutish person

Bogged   vehicle stuck in the sand or mud

Boiler   an old woman

Bomb   1. run-down car; 2. make a large splash when jumping into a pool

Bomb   3. fail a test; 4. something very cool; 5. spray with graffiti

Boney   very thin, emaciated

Bonkers   out of control, crazy

Bonnet   car's front engine cover, hood

Bonzer   excellent, good

Boogie board   small surfboard, body board

Bookie   a bookmaker

Boomer   a large kangaroo

Boomerang   an Aboriginal weapon

Boot   car rear luggage compartment, trunk

The **bog house**, **dunny** or **thunder box** was found in most **Aussie** backyards until the mid 20th Century.

Booze   alcoholic drink

Booze bus   vehicle used for assessing a driver's blood alcohol concentration

Boozer   1. a pub or hotel; 2. a person who is a heavy drinker

Bored shitless   extremely bored

Boss cocky   an employer

Bottle shop   liquor store

Bottle-o   liquor store, bottle shop

Bottler   excellent!

Bottling, your blood's worth   a compliment of very special praise

Bouncer   a person employed to evict troublemakers

Bower bird   a collector of trash and many objects

Bozo   idiot

Brass   money, cash

Brass monkey, freeze the balls off a   very cold

Brass razoo, he hasn't got a   he is very poor

Breaker   a person who breaks in horses

Brekkie   breakfast

Brickie   a brick layer

Bring a plate   bring a plate of food to a party or barbeque

Brisvegas   Brisbane, state capital of Queensland

Brizzie   Brisbane, state capital of Queensland

Broke   no money

Brown eye   expose one's anus or bum

Brown nose   suck up to the boss, crawler, boot licker

Brumby   wild Australian horse

Bub   1. baby; 2. affectionate name for one's girlfriend or wife

Buck's night   stag party, male gathering on the eve before a wedding

Buckley's/Buckley's chance   no chance at all

Buddy   mate, pal

Budgie   budgerigar

Budgie smugglers   men's bathing costume
Bugger   1. person; 2. annoying person, nuisance; 3. cause inconvenience
Bugger all   very little amount
Bugger off   go away
Buggered   1. broken; 2. very tired
Built   good physique, well built
Built like a brick shit house   solidly built
Bull bar   a bar fixed to a vehicle to protect it against hitting wildlife
Bull dust   a lie
Bull shit   unbelievable statement
Bum   1. buttocks; 2. tramp; 3. get for nothing; 4. mild annoyance
Bum fluff   facial hair growth on a teenage male
Bum nuts   eggs
Bum steer   false information
Bundy   Bundaberg, Queensland and the rum that is produced there
Bung   1. damaged, broken; 2. place or put without care; 3. stopper
Bunyip   a mythical creature
Burl   try something
Burn   drive at high speed
Bush   rural Australia
Bush bash   to travel off road in a vehicle
Bushie   a person from the bush
Bushranger   an outlaw
Bush telegraph   gossip network
Bush whacker   a derogatory term for a person from the outback
Butcher   a small glass of beer in South Australia
Butcher's hook   cook or chef
By jingoes   exclamation of wonder
Cab sav   cabernet sauvignon wine
Cabbie   taxi driver

Cack   defecate
Cackelberry   egg
Cactus   broken, not working
Cadge   beg or borrow
Cagey   shy, wary
Cahoots   in partnership
Cake hole   mouth
Camp as a row of tents   a male homosexual
Camp oven   cast iron cooking pot
Can   a prison
Can of worms   problems, troublesome
Cancer stick   cigarette
Can-do   affirmative, yes
Cane toad   a person from Queensland
Caper   activity
Captain Cook   look
Carbie/Carby   carburetor
Cardie   cardigan
Cark it   to die
Carnie   carnival worker
Cash and carry   a supermarket
Cashed up   plenty of money
Chalkie   a school teacher
Champers   champagne
Chancy   uncertain, risky
Charge like a wounded bull   to charge excessively high prices
Cheese and kisses   wife
Cheesed off   very angry, annoyed
Cherry   a red cricket ball
Chew the fat   have a chat or conversation

Cooking in a **camp oven** is part of **Aussie outback** history and today the **camp oven** is used by campers.

Chewie   chewing gum

Chiack   taunt, tease

Chicken shit   no value, worthless

China plate   mate, pal, friend

Chin wag   have a chat, conversation

Chippie   a carpenter, wood worker

Chips   potato fries, crisps

Chock a block/Chockers   very full, overflowing

Chockie   chocolate

Chockie bikkies   chocolate biscuits

Choke a brown dog   something distasteful, bad food

Choof off   go now, get lost, leave

Chook   a chicken or fowl

Choppers   teeth, false teeth

Chrissie   Christmas time

Some **Aussies** still prefer to keep **chooks** in their backyards to provide **googies** rather than buy them from the grocery shop.

Chrome dome   a bald man

Chuck   1. throw, toss; 2. vomit

Chuck a sickie   take a work sick day when you're not sick

Chuck it in   quit, give up, surrender

Chuffed   very happy

Chunder   to vomit

Clackers   false teeth

Clanger   1. a big lie; 2. a shock

Clapped out   worn out, old

Classer   a wool grader

Claytons   fake

Cleanskin   1. a bottle of wine without a label; 2. unbranded cattle

Clear as mud   confusing

Clever dick   1. a smart person; 2. a conceited person

Clicks, Klicks, K's   kilometres

Clink   prison
Clobber   clothes
Clod hoppers   feet
Clucky, feeling   broody, maternal
Coat hanger   Sydney Harbour bridge
Cobber   work mate, friend, pal
Cock up   something gone wrong
Cockie   1. cockatoo; 2. farmer, grazier; 3. cockroach
Cocky's joy   golden syrup, treacle
Codger   a perculiar person, unusual
Cods   testicles
Coit   bum, anus
Coldie   a beer bottle or can

Cockies are cold-blooded pests who thrive in warm, humid conditions. They make their home wherever they find food, moisture and shelter.

Colonial goose   a boned leg of lamb seasoned with herbs and onion
Come a gutser   1. have an accident; 2. to make a mistake
Come in spinner   call for the tossing of the coins in the game of two-up
Come the raw prawn   pretend, be naive
Come to blows   start fighting
Common as dog shit   very common
Compo   workers compensation payment
Conk   nose
Conk out   engine breakdown
Conned   tricked, deceived
Cooee   a call; often used in the bush to locate lost persons
Cook   one's wife
Cooking with gas   doing very well
Cop   1. police officer; 2. obtain; 3. caught doing something wrong
Corker   something astonishing or striking
Corroboree   a ceremonial meeting of Australian Aborigines
Cossie   swimming costume

Couldn't lie straight in bed a cheat, liar
Counter lunch/countery pub lunch
Country cousin a dozen, twelve
Cove a man, bloke or chap
Cow cocky dairy farmer
Cow of a thing frustrating or upsetting
Crack a fat get an erection
Crack of dawn first light of day
Crack onto make a pass or pursue someone romantically
Cracker the tip of a stock whip
Cranky angry, in a bad mood
Creamed soundly beaten in sport
Creek a small stream
Crikey an expression of astonishment
Crim a criminal
Croak to die
Croc crocodile
Crook 1. unwell; 2. no good, bad, rotten
Crook as Rookwood sick (Rookwood being a cemetery)
Cropper, came a fall over
Crow bar a large lever
Crow eater a South Australian
Crown jewels testicles
Crud dirt, rubbish
Cruet the head
Cubby house a small house made for children to play in
Cunning as a shit house rat a very cunning person
Cuppa a cup of tea or coffee
Curly nickname for a bald person
Cut lunch sandwiches or pre-packed lunch

Australia has two different species of **crocs**, both of which are native to tropical Queensland.

Cut snake, mad as a   1. very upset; 2. crazy
Cut the crap   stop talking rubbish
Cut up   1. upset, distressed; 2. criticise
Dab hand at   good at, skilled
Dacks/Daks   1.trousers, pants; 2. underpants
Dad and Dave   a shave
Daddy long legs   a long-legged spider
Dag   1. an amusing person; 2. dry excreta hanging from a sheep's wool
Daggy   1. untidy; 2. dirty; 3. uncool, lacking style
Dago   war-time name for Italians
Daily grind   monotonous work
Dakka   marijuana, pot, dope
Damper   bread made from flour and water usually cooked in a camp oven
Dangle   to die by hanging, to hang
Dangle the carrot   offer a bribe, tempt
Darl   darling
Dart   a cigarette
Darwin shuffle   tax avoidance scheme
Darwin stubbie   a very large beer bottle
Date   anus
Date roller   roll of toilet paper
Dazzler   brilliant, good
Dead as mutton   very dead
Dead beat   very tired

Uluru is situated in the **dead heart** of Australia.

Dead heart   the arid centre of Australia
Dead horse   tomato sauce
Dead marine   empty beer bottle
Dead on   correct
Dead ringer   a close resemblance of someone else
Dead set   correct, spot on, a sure thing

Deadbeat   1. loser, lazy person; 2. one who doesn't pay their debts
Deadly   fantastic, great, awesome
Dee   a detective
Demo   a demonstration
Dero/Derro   a derelict, vagrant dependant on alcohol
Dial   your face
Dibs   marbles
Dice   throw away, reject
Dicey   unreliable
Dickhead   jerk, annoying person, idiot
Dickory dock   clock
Diddle   to cheat, swindle
Diddler   swindler
Dig me   I've done well, excelled
Dig you   you've done well, excelled
Digger   an Australian soldier
Dill   a stupid person
Dilly bag   a small bag to carry sugar, tea, etc
Ding   a minor motor accident
Ding bat   a fool, silly person
Ding dong   a major fight
Dinger   anus, backside
Dingo   an Australian native dog
Dink   to carry a second person on a bike, motorcycle or horse
Dinky-di   the genuine article
Dinkum   no joke, the real thing
Dip out   1. miss out; 2. to refuse a drink
Dipstick   idiot, a loser
Divvy up   share out equally
Dob in   1. tell on someone, report; 2. contribute to a fund

The **Dingo** is **Oz's** wild dog. It is medium in size with a red to yellow coat and bushy tail. **Dingos** don't bark but they howl.

Docket   receipt, bill

Doco   a documentary

Dodgy   something suspicious

Dog and bone   phone

Dog box   a compartment in a train carriage

Dog fence   to keep dingoes out of pastoral country

Dogger   a dingo hunter

Dog's balls, stands out like   very obvious

Dog's breakfast   a real mess, confusion, turmoil

Dog's eye   a meat pie

Dole   social security payment

A **dog's eye** is a small meat pie often containing minced or diced meat and gravy. Sometimes smothered with **dead horse**, it is an iconic **Aussie takeaway** food snack.

Dole bludger   won't work and being supported by the government

Dolled up   women dressed smartly

Done like a dinner   beaten in sport or a fight

Donga/Donger   a penis

Donk   a boat or car engine

Doodle   a penis

Doona   duvet

Doovalacky   used when you can't remember what something is called

Doover   1. a penis; 2. a thing

Dork   1. a penis; 2. someone who is uncool

Dose, a   venereal disease

Down a few   have a few drinks

Down the hatch   drink up

Down under   Australia

Drag Queen   transvestite, dresses as a woman

Drag the chain   to be slow, lag behind

Dray   a wagon, horse cart

Driza-bone   a weatherproof coat or jacket

Drongo   a stupid person

Drop a fart   to pass wind
Drop kick   a useless person
Drop your guts   to fart
Drover   stock moving contractor, stockman
Drum   1. give information or advice; 2. to organise
Dry as a dead dingo's donger   very dry, thirsty
Dry rots   diarrhoea, the trots
Duchess   dressing table, sideboard
Duck's guts   a very good thing
Duckshove   pass responsibilities off to others
Dudds   male clothing
Duff   1. mess up; 2. steal cattle
Duff, up the   pregnant
Duffer   stupid person, unthinking
Duffing   stealing cattle or sheep
Dummy, spit the   have a tantrum
Dump   1. poorly kept house; 2. act of defecation; 3. end a relationship
Dumper   a large wave breaking onto a beach
Dunny   a toilet; indoor or outdoor
Dunny diver   a plumber
Dunny paper   toilet paper
Durry   a cigarette
Dust up   brawl or fight
Dutch oven   farting under the bed sheets
Dux   top of the class
Eager beaver   a keen person
Eagle eyes   very good eyesight
Eagle hawking   plucking wool from dead sheep
Eagle shits   getting paid
Ear bashing   persistent talking, nagging

Toilet paper is referred to as **dunny paper** however, in the early days, most **dunny paper** was actually torn up sheets of newspaper.

Earful   1. oral advice; 2. stern reprimand
Early bird   1. get up early; 2. arrive early
Early mark   leave work before normal finishing time
Earn a quid   working for a living, making money
Ears flapping   eavesdropping, listening in
Easy   1. to have no firm preference; 2. promiscuous
Easy lay   a woman with loose morals
Easy-peasy   very easy
Eat a horse   very hungry
Eat a horse and chase the rider   indicating one's great hunger
Eat crow   embarrassment when a plan has failed or backfired
Edgy   nervous
Egg beater   helicopter
Egg head   an intellectual person
Ekka   the Brisbane Agricultural Exhibition
Elbow grease   hard work
El-cheapo   1. something very cheap; 2. inferior quality
Elevator   lift
Emcee   master of ceremony
Empties   empty beer bottles
Emu   a racecourse person who picks up discarded betting tickets
Emu-bobber   someone employed to pick up rubbish after a function
Emu parade   group of people employed to clean up after large gatherings
Entree   appetiser, starter
Enzed/NZ   an acronym, New Zealand
Enzedder   a New Zealander
Esky   a portable insulated container used to keep food and drink cool
Even stevens   1. equal; 2. not owed anything
Even the score   revenge
Every dog has its day   opportunities come your way

Every man and his dog   a general public crowd
Every Tom, Dick and Harry   a general public crowd
Every which way   all directions
Ex   one's former wife, husband, girlfriend or boyfriend
Exchange notes   to gossip
Excuse the French   apology for bad language
Expecting   pregnant
Exy   expensive
Eye off   to look at with interest
Eyeball to eyeball   face to face

Every Tom, Dick and Harry was at the opening of the new shopping centre.

Eyes like road maps   bloodshot after a big night out
Eyesore   offensive, ugly
FJ   a popular model of the Holden car 1953-1956
Fab   fabulous, wonderful, great
Face ache   irritating person
Face fungus   a beard
Face like a festered pimple   1. acute acne; 2. ugly
Face, off one's   drunk
Fag   1. a cigarette; 2. a homosexual
Fagged out   tired
Fair and square   honest, trustworthy
Fair crack of the whip   to be treated fairly, asking for a fair chance
Fair dinkum   real, true
Fair enough   agreeing about something
Fair go mate   give a chance
Fair suck of the sav   1. a fair go; 2. exclamation of wonder or disbelief
Fairy   homosexual male
Fairy floss   cotton candy, candy floss
Falsies   1. fake breasts; 2. false teeth
Famished   very hungry

Fangs   teeth
Fanny   a vagina
Far flung   remote, far away
Fart sack   1. a bed or bunk; 2. a sleeping bag
Fart-arse   waste time
Farts like a two-stroke   loud flatulence
Fat cake   damper fried in fat
Favourite poison   preferred alcoholic drink
Feel crook   unwell
Feel horny   sexually aroused
Fell off the back of a truck   stolen property
Fella   a male person
Feral   a hippie
Fergie/Fergy   a Ferguson tractor
Ferret   a penis
Few and far between   rare, not common
Fib   a lie, untruth
Fibber   a liar
Fiddle   to cheat
Fiddler   a swindler
Fifty-fifty   equal amounts
Figjam   *uck I'm good just ask me; high opinion of oneself
Filly   1. a young girl; 2. female horse
Filthy rich   very wealthy
Finicky   fastidious
Fins   the arms
Fire away   begin to speak
Fire blanks   a sterile male
Firebug   arsonist
First cab off the rank   first in line

Feral Meryl believes the way to peace is through love and tolerance.

First fleeter   a person who can be traced back to the first fleet
First thing   early morning
Fish out of water   uncomfortable with other people or surroundings
Fisho   a fishmonger
Fit as a mallee bull   a very fit person
Fits like a glove   suitable, a good fit
Five o'clock shadow   beard growth on a man's face
Five finger discount   shop lifting
Fizzer   1. a failure; 2. fiasco
Flak   criticism
Flake   shark's flesh; commonly sold in fish and chip shops
Flake out   lie down, to sleep
Flame   girlfriend, sweetheart
Flamin'   1. very good; 2. very bad
Flap your gums   talk too much
Flash a brown eye   expose ones bare backside, anus
Flasher   a man who exposes his genitals in public

Fred the **flasher.**

Flat as a tack   1. tired, worn out; 2. anything that is flat
Flat broke   having no money
Flat chat   as fast as possible
Flat out like a lizard drinking   a very busy person, working hard
Flatfoot   a policeman
Flatties   low-heeled shoes
Flea bag   infested with fleas
Flea-house   cinema, picture theatre
Flesh and blood   family, kin, offspring
Flick   1. getting rid of something; 2. movie
Flick it on   sell something soon after buying for a quick profit
Flippers   hands
Floater   1. a meat pie in a plate of gravy; 2. faeces floating in a toilet

Flog   1. to sell something; 2. to steal something

Flogging a dead horse   trying to do something when it won't work

Floozie   a promiscuous woman

Fluke   to win by chance

Flunk   to fail

Flutter   place a small bet

Fly the coop   1. escape; 2. leave home

Flyblown   maggots on meat

Flying fox   a cable car

Fob off   1. dismiss; 2. be rude to someone

Foggiest   no idea or clue

Snowy took **forty winks** during **smoko** because he couldn't keep his **peepers** open.

Fool's gold   pyrites; a mineral that resembles gold

Foot the bill   pay the costs

Footpath   sidewalk

Footslogger   a soldier

Footy   term for Australian rules football, rugby league or rugby union

For keeps   permanently own

Fork over   pay a bet, hand over something

Forty winks   a short nap or sleep

Fossick   search for gold or gemstones

Fossil   an old person

Foulmouthed   using obscene language

Four eyes   a person who wears glasses

Four letter word   any vulgar words having four letters

Four-b-two/four   a piece of timber

Foursome   four people in a party

Franger   a condom

Freckle   the anus

Fred Nerk   an imaginary person

Free loader   a person who uses somebody's hospitality, food and drink

Freebie   something for nothing
Free-for-all   a fight involving many people
Freeze the balls off a brass monkey   very cold, frosty
Fremantle Doctor   Perth breeze from the direction of Fremantle
Frenchie   a condom
Freo   Fremantle, Western Australia
Freshie   a fresh water crocodile
Fridge   a refrigerator
Fried eggs   flat breasts
Frig   to masturbate
Frigging   masturbating
Frigid   an unresponsive person
Frillie   a frill-necked lizard
Fringe benefit   extra rewards above regular wage
Frisky   sexually aroused
Frog   a French person
Frog and toad   road
Frogshit   insincere talk, nonsense
From a to z   from the beginning to the end
From arsehole to breakfast time   1. all over; 2. completely covered
From go to whoa   from the beginning to the end
From pillar to post   roaming from one place to another
From scratch   from nothing
Fruit for the sideboard   perks, rewards, bonus
Fruitloop   a crazy person
Fuddy-duddy   1. conservative; 2. a fussy person
Full as a boot   very drunk, intoxicated
Full bore   to go all out
Full frontal   a naked body from front on
Full of beans   very energetic

The **fridge** was absolutely **chockers** with drinks and **tucker**.

Full of shit talking rubbish
Full on most intense
Full quid sane
Fungus face a male with a beard
Furphy 1. originally a water cart; 2. a rumour or a false report, a lie
Fuss pot 1. a person who worries a lot; 2. a very fussy person
Fuzz the police
Fuzzy-headed a bad hangover
Fuzzy wuzzy angel WWII stretcher bearer from Papua New Guinea
G'day/Gidday Good-day, hello
Ga Ga mad, silly
Gab chatter, talk
Gabba Queensland Cricket Ground at Wooloongabba, Brisbane
Gadabout a person having an active social life
Gag a joke
Galah 1. native Australian parrot; 2. a fool, idiot
Gallops thoroughbred horse races
Galoot a stupid clumsy person
Galvo galvanized iron
Game as a piss ant a very daring person
Game as Ned Kelly very daring
Games up the end of an activity
Gammy crippled, lame
Gander have a look at something
Gangie group sex
Ganja marijuana
Gaol bird habitual criminal
Garbage guts a greedy person
Garbo garbage or waste collector
Gas bagging talk at great length non-stop.

Ned Kelly is an **Aussie** folk hero yet he was a criminal. He is remembered today in the popular expression, "as **game as Ned Kelly**".

Gasper   a cigarette

Gawk   stare openly

Gear   clothes, uniform

Gee gee   a horse

Geek   have a look

Genny   a generator

Gents   a public toilet for men only

German band   your hand

Get a bit   have sexual intercourse

Get a dose   contract a venereal disease

Get a leg in the door   make headway

Get a wriggle on   hurry up

Get nicked   exclamation of contempt

Get off at Redfern   withdraw before ejaculation

Get rooted   a term of abuse; go away!

Get stuffed   a term of abuse; go away, piss off!

Get stuck into   1. abuse someone; 2. eat hungrily; 3. do a task with vigour

Get the arse   to be fired/sacked

Get the big A   to be fired/sacked

Get the nod   get approval, the go ahead

Get the rough end of the pineapple   worst treatment

Get the shits   get upset

Gibber   a round stone, a small rock

Gig   1. performance at a venue; 2. gigabyte

Gimme   give me

Give the game away   to abandon interest

Give it a burl   to try, have a go

Give it a miss   change one's mind

Give lip   cheeky, answer back

Glad rags   your best clothes

Jo and Flo spent most of the day **gas bagging** about the new **bloke** at the office.

Glass of amber   a glass of beer

Go ape shit   become very angry

Go bad   1. down on one's luck; 2. a bad joke that is not appreciated

Go down like a lead balloon   failure

Go Dutch   pay your own way

Go for a burn   1. to drive fast; 2. test drive

Go for a snake hiss   a male to urinate

Go like the clappers   move fast

Go off half-cocked   not thinking straight

Go to buggery   ask someone to leave in a very nasty way

Go walkabout   wandering off

Goanna   a piano

Gob   mouth

Gobful, give a   to abuse

Gobsmacked   astounded, flabbergasted

Goer   1. an energetic person; 2. go ahead with something

Going off   used to describe a fun night spot or party

Gone to billyo   disappeared

Gone to the dogs   going from good to bad

Good as gold   something very good

Good monger   good food

Good oil   correct information

Good on ya   well done

Good sort   a good looking woman

Goog, as full as a   1. drunk; 2. full of food

Googie   an egg

Goolies   testicles

Goss   gossip

Grab forty winks   have a nap

Grazier   pastoral property owner

Nothing beats a boiled
googie for **brekkie**.

Greasy a bad cook

Great Australian salute the action of shooing flies away with your hand

Green around the gills feeling sick

Green thumb able to make any plant grow

Greenie an environmentalist

Grizzle to complain

Grog alcohol

Grommet a teenage surfer

Grot an untidy person

Grouse very good, terrific

Grub 1. food; 2. a meal; 3. a dirty eater; 4. a dirty child

Grundies underwear (from television and media mogul, Reg Grundy)

Grunt power, strength

Gully a very small valley

Gummies gumboots

Gun 1. best at something; 2. accelerate a vehicle

Gunna all talk and no action

Gunyah an aboriginal shelter

Gutful had enough

Gutful of piss drunk

Gutsy brave, fearsome

Guttersnipe a gossiper

Gutzer to fall over, trip

Guzzler a heavy drinker

Gyno a gynecologist

Barry **hoed into** a big plate of **grub** for **tea**.

Hack 1. a taxi; 2. horse

Had a few too many too many alcoholic drinks

Had a good innings a good life

Had a skin full drinks too much

Had it 1. run out of patience; 2. dead

Had it soft   an easy time
Hair of the dog   a drink to cure a hangover
Half shot   nearly intoxicated
Half time   the middle of a team sport's game
Half your luck   very lucky
Half-mast   trousers that don't reach the ankles
Ham and eggs   legs
Hammer and tongs   worked very hard
Hammy   hamstring
Hand   a hired worker
Hand in hand   worked together
Hand in the till   stealing from employer
Hand the hat around   giving to a cause
Hand-me-downs   passed on clothing
Handy   skilled, clever
Hang around like a bad smell   not wanted around
Hang on a tick   wait a minute
Hanger-on   a free loader
Hankie   handkerchief
Happy as a pig in shit   very happy
Happy as Larry   extremely happy
Happy little vegemite   someone in a good mood
Hard word on   1. to ask a favour; 2. to ask a sexual favour
Hassle   1. a problem; 2. inconvenience
Hate someone's guts   dislike someone
Haul   ill gotten goods
Haunt   favourite place
Have a ball   a very good time
Have a bang   have sexual intercourse
Have a barney   a fight

Have a bo-peep   have a look
Have a burl   attempt something
Have a crack   attempt
Have a decko/dekko   have a look
Have a domestic   a family argument
Have a flutter   a small bet, wager
Have a gander   have a look
Have a go   try something
Have a heart   have mercy
Have a pash   long, passionate kiss
Have a prang   car smash, accident
Have a shot at   to try something
Have a snort   have an alcoholic drink
Have a spell   a rest from work
Have a splash   have a bet, wager
Have a stab at   attempt something
Have a tub   bath or wash

Bluey decided to **have a tub** to soothe his aching body after a day of hard **yakka**.

Have long arms and short pockets   to be a miser, stingy
Haven't got a brass razoo   broke, no money
Hayburner   a horse
Head in the sand   to ignore reality
Heads and tails   used in the game of two-up
Heaps   a lot, a large amount
Heard it all before   same thing over and over
Heart of gold   1. generous; 2. helpful
Heart of stone   mean, unemotional
Heart starter   early morning alcoholic drink, strong coffee, first cigarette
Heart stopper   shocking, terrifying
Heavies   minders, bodyguards
Heebie-jeebies   tension, nervousness

Heifers   young female cattle
Hell for leather   fast, speeding
Hemp   marijuana
Hen-pecked   dominated by a wife
Hen's night   bachelorette party
Hen's teeth   scarce
Here to stay   permanent
Herk   vomit
Hey   greeting
Hick   country person
Hickey   a love bite
Hidey hole   a secret hiding place
High and dry   abandoned, alone
High as a kite   1. under the influence of drugs or alcohol; 2. in high spirits
High flying   doing well in business
High on the nose   stinking, smelly
Highfaluting   snobbish, pompous, pretentious
His nibs   the boss, one in charge
Hit and giggle   tennis
Hit and miss   careless
Hit the frog and toad   depart
Hit the hay   go to bed
Hit the headlines   achieve fame
Hit the jackpot   very lucky
Hit the nail on the head   exactly right
Hit the piss   drink heavily
Hit the roof   become angry
Hit the sack   go to bed
Hit the slops   get on the booze
Hit the toe   depart, go

Jack **hit the slops** every night at his local **watering hole** before heading home to **cop** an **ear bashing** from the **ball and chain**.

Hiya greeting
Hobbles straps used to tie horses' legs
Hoe into start eating
Hold the reins be in charge
Hollies/Hols holidays
Holy dooley exclamation indicating surprise, indignation
Holy mackerel exclamation indicating surprise, indignation
Holy smoke exclamation indicating surprise, indignation
Home and hosed easy winner; foregone conclusion, successful finish
Homely 1. plain; 2. cosy, snug
Homestead the main house on a property
Homo a homosexual man
Honk 1. the nose; 2. blow a car's horn
Honkers Hong Kong
Hooch marijuana
Hoof it to walk, run
Hooks fingers
Hooley a wild party
Hoon a reckless show off
Hoop a jockey
Hooray 1. goodbye; 2. pleasure
Hooroo goodbye
Hop it go away
Hopping mad very angry
Hops beer
Horn 1. an erection; 2. a telephone
Horn in enter a discussion uninvited
Horse and cart a fart
Horse around play up
Horse sense common sense

Bazza was **hopping mad**
when he noticed that some
galoot had **pranged** into
the side of his new car.

Horse play   rough behaviour

Horses for courses   suited to the task

Horse's hoof   homosexual

Hostie   air hostess, flight attendant

Hot air   pretentious, empty talk

Hot to trot   eager to start

Hot foot it   go, depart, leave

Hot pants   a woman with strong sexual desires

Hot under the collar   very angry

Hotel   a pub

Hottie   1. a hot water bottle; 2. a sexy person

House of ill fame   a brothel

How about it?   asking for sex

How come?   why

How ya goin?   greeting

How's it going?   greeting

How's things?   greeting

Howzat?   an appeal for approval

Hoy   attract attention

Hubby   husband

According to **every Tom, Dick and Harry**, Brenda was a **bloody bonzer hostie** and a real **hottie.**

Huey   another name for God, the powers above

Humbug   1. a striped lolly; 2. a cheat

Humdinger   very good, the best

Hump   1. carry something; 2. lift; 3. have sex

Humpy   a rough bush shelter

Hung over   feeling poorly after a drinking binge

Hurl   vomit

Husband beater   a rolling pin

Hush money   a bribe

Hush up   keep quiet

Hustle   to obtain money illegally
Hype   overdone
Hyped up/Hypo   over excited
I.O.U   "I owe you", a written confirmation of debt
I kid you not   declaration that one is speaking the truth
I'll be   exclamation of surprise
I'll drink to that   agree, approve
I'm all right Jack   ok
I've had it   complete frustration
Ice block/Icy pole   popsicle
Icing on the cake   best finish
Icky   1. offensive; 2. risky
Idiot box   a television set
Idle rich   very wealthy people
Iffy   suspicious
Illywhacker   a small time trickster, crook
Imp   a naughty child
In a jiff/jiffy   soon, a short time
In a spin   confused
In a spot of bother   in trouble
In a tic   soon
In cloudland   not concentrating
In cog   in disguise, incognito
In droves   big numbers
In fine feathers   full of vitality
In fits and starts   irregular
In for the kill   defeat
In good nick   good condition
In hock   in debt
In house   associated to members of a house or club

An **ice block** is a sweet cold
confection consisting of ice
cream or flavoured water
frozen on a stick.

In like Flynn   1. a sure thing; 2. sexual success (referring to Errol Flynn)
In strife   in trouble
In the bag   success
In the box seat   successful position
In the can   in prison
In the chair   next to buy a round of drinks
In the clink   in gaol
In the cooler   in gaol
In the cot   in bed
In the doghouse   out of favour with your wife, husband or partner
In the drink   in water
In the family way   pregnant
In the good books   in favour
In the grip of the grape   addicted to wine
In the guts   in the centre, middle
In the know   inside information
In the nuddy   naked
In the raw   naked, nude
In the red   in debt
In the right place at the right time   in a good position
In the same boat   in the same situation, face the same challenges
In the shit   in serious trouble
In the sticks   remote areas in the bush
In the wars   1. minor injuries; 2. arguments
In tow   following someone
In trouble   pregnant
Indian giver   give a gift to someone then take it back
Info   information
In-laws   relatives by marriage
Inside job   a crime within an organisation

Into thin air   disappear
Intro   introduction
Irish curtains   cobwebs
Iron clad   safe
Iron fisted   ruthless, severe
Iron oneself out   get drunk
Iron underpants   girdles, step-ins
Irrits   the shits
Is it a goer?   will it happen?
Is the Pope Catholic?   yes
It   could be male or female
It's a goer   1. will happen; 2. proceed
It's in the cards   may happen
It's sweet   all is ok
It's your funeral   your fault
It never rains but it pours   lots of things happen at once
Itchy feet   need to travel
Itsy-bitsy   very small, tiny
Ivories   teeth, false teeth
J.P.   a Justice of the Peace
Jab   an injection
Jabber   to talk rapidly
Jack dancer   cancer
Jack in the box   someone who cannot sit still
Jack of all trades   someone who can do all jobs
Jacked off   1. annoyed; 2. disgusted; 3. frustrated
Jack Shay   to stay
Jack shit   nothing
Jack up   1. refuse to work; 2. disobey
Jackass   1. kookaburra; 2. an idiot

Yes, the Pope is Catholic.

Jacked off   1. annoyed; 2. masturbated
Jackeroo   a male stock hand
Jackie/Jacky   kookaburra
Jacky Howe   a sleeveless garment worn by labourers
Jaffle   a toasted sandwich
Jake   okay, alright
Jam tart   sweetheart
Jammed in   over-crowded
Jargon   nonsense, meaningless talk
Jarmies   pyjamas, night dress
Jay-cee   Jesus Christ
Jelly   1. gelatin desert, jello; 2. gelignite, explosive
Jerk   a fool
Jerkin the gherkin   to masturbate
Jerry built   badly built
Jiffy   very short time
Jiggered   broken, spoiled
Jillaroo   a female stock hand
Jimmy Woodser   a person who drinks on their own in a bar
Jingoes   exclamation of surprise
Jittery   nervous, anxious
Job somebody   to hit someone, fight
Jock   genital support worn by sportsmen
Jockeys   male underpants
Jocks   male underpants
Joe Blake   a snake
Joe Bloggs   anybody
Joe Blow   an ordinary bloke
Joey   baby kangaroo
John   1. a policeman; 2. a toilet; 3. prostitute's client

J

Johnny cake   1. damper; 2. bush cakes
Johnny come lately   a recent arrival
Join up   enlist for military service
Joint   a house, place, abode
Joker   1. a person who is amusing; 2. a person you're unsure about
Jollies   sexual excitement
Jonah   to bring bad luck
Journo   a journalist
Joy ride   an enjoyable ride
Jug   1. prison; 2. measure of beer served in a large glass jug
Juggle the pennies   budget
Jugs   breasts, boobs
Juice   petrol, gas
Jumble sale   a sale of second-hand items
Jumbuck   a sheep
Jump at it   1. chance it; 2. offered a job
Jump bail   abscond after paying bail
Jump in and out of bed   be very promiscuous
Jump in the lake   go away, piss off
Jump start   get a good start
Jump the gun   start too soon
Jump the queue   jump in front of someone in line
Jump the rattler   ride the train illegally
Jumper   1. sweater, pullover; 2. commit suicide by jumping from a height
Jump up and down   1. make a fuss; 2. strongly protest
Jumpy   nervous, tense
Jungle juice   home-made inferior alcoholic drink
Junk   anything that is worthless
Junk food   take-away food
Jump the gun   gain an unfair advantage by starting prematurely

Jumbuck is an **Aussie** term for sheep and is featured in the famous poem and song, "Waltzing Matilda".

Just down the street   not far away
Just my luck   frustration
Just what the doctor ordered   exactly what is required
K's   kilometres
Kafuffle   a commotion
Kamikaze   a reckless act
Kanaka   a Pacific Islander (seldom used)
Kanakas   testicles
Kanga   1. kangaroo; 2. shoe
Kaput   1. broken, smashed; 2. is dead
Kark   1. die; 2. broken, ruined
Keel over   1. to fall over; 2. die; 3. faint
Keen as mustard   very enthusiastic
Keen on someone   attracted to someone
Keep a low profile   keep away from publicity
Keep an eye on everything   watch over, look after
Keep back   restrain, withhold
Keep in touch   maintain a friendship
Keep it in the family   keep secrets within a family
Keep on the ball   constant alertness
Keep one's chin up   maintain good spirits, courage
Keep one's head above water   survive at all costs
Keep one's mouth shut   refrain from speaking out
Keep your shirt on   settle down, take it easy
Keg   a barrel of beer
Kelpie   an Australian sheepdog
Kero   kerosene
Khyber pass   arse, bum
Kick   1. pleasurable thrill; 2. strong alcohol taste; 3. trouser pocket
Kick arse   totally amazing

Kick back   relax

Kick in   1. to contribute; 2. buy a drink

Kick in the arse   a severe scolding

Kick in the teeth   a severe setback

Kick off   commence to play sport; football, soccer

Kick on   to continue

Kick the bucket   to die

Kick the tin   1. donate; 2. buy a round of drinks

Kick up one's heels   have fun

Kiddo   to address a young person

Kicking up a shinty   making an angry fuss

Kill a brown dog   potent, deadly

Kill a snake   urinate

Kill the goose that lays the golden eggs   end something profitable

Killer, a   a sheep or cow killed for meat on a property

Kimberley cool   the coolness beer reaches when immersed in a water bag

Kimberley formal   men's dress style; shirt, shorts, socks and shoes

Kimberley mutton   wild goat roasted

Kindie   kindergarten

King Dick   1. the best; 2. above ordinary people

King hit   a surprise punch in the head

King pin   a boss or leader

Kink   1. a cramp, twinge; 2. a sexual pervert

Kinky   unusual sexual tastes

Kip   1. a small thin piece of flat wood used to toss coins in a game of two-up

Kip   2. a short sleep

Kiwi   a New Zealander

Klicks   kilometres

Knackered   very tired

Knackers   testicles

Knee high to a grasshopper   a short person

Knee trembler   1. frightening; 2. sexual intercourse standing up

Knickers   underpants for women

Knick knacks   trinkets, bric a brac

Knife in the back   a betrayal

Knob   1. penis; 2. annoying or stupid person, dickhead

Knock   to criticise

Knock back   1. a refusal, a rebuff; 2. consume a drink

Knock down   1. reduce the price; 2. spend freely on liquor

Knock it off   1. stop it!; 2. euphemism for sexual intercourse

Knock off   1. stop work; 2. steal something; 3. make a copy

Knock shop   a brothel

Knock up   1. make pregnant; 2. construct; 3. cook hastily; 4. exhaust

Knocked up   pregnant

Knocker   one who derides all ideas, things and projects

Knuckle down   show willing to work

Knuckle sandwich   a bunch of fives, a punch to the teeth

Knuckle, to go the   to fight, to punch

Kombi   a small van, wagon

Konk   nose

Koori   an aborigine

Kosher   the real thing

Kybosh   rubbish, nonsense

Lab   laboratory

Lace into   attack, abuse

Ladies   womens' toilet

Ladies man   a man attracted to women

Lady muck   a snobby woman

Lady's waist   either a 5 or 7 ounce glass of beer

Lag   a habitual criminal, convict

Dave discovered that Gary had been **eyeing off** his **flame** and threatened him with a **knuckle sandwich**.

Lagerphone   a musical instrument made of bottle tops nailed to a stick

Lagger   a police informer

Laid up   sick, bedridden

Laid back   relaxed

Lair/Lairy   1. a flashy male; 2. vulgar person; 3. show off

Lamington   small square sponge cake coated in chocolate icing and coconut

Lappy   a laptop

Larrikin   a prankster, hooligan

Lash at, have a   to make an attempt at something

Lash out   1. spend freely; 2. burst into violent action or criticise severely

Last resort   a final option

Laugh at the lawn   to vomit

Laughing gear   the mouth

Laughing jackass   a kookaburra

Lav/Lavvy   outdoor toilet, any toilet

Lay   a person considered as a sex object, a good lay

Lay a cable   to defecate

Lay down the law   what I say goes, the boss

Lay in the hay   have sexual intercourse

Lay into   to beat up, abuse

Lay low   stay out of site

Lay off   1. ease up, stop; 2. be sacked

Layabout   a lazy person

Lenny the **larrikin** had a real **lead foot** and would **go like the clappers** around town.

Lay-down misere   it's a certainty

Lazy Susan   a revolving centre tray on a dining table

Lead a dog's life   an unhappy life

Lead feet/foot   to drive too fast, a reckless driver

Leak   to urinate

Learner   a person learning to drive a motor vehicle

Leave it at that   end of story, say no more in conversation

Left to the wolves   deserted
Left footer   a Catholic
Leg it   to walk or run
Legal eagle   a lawyer or solicitor
Legless   very drunk
Lemon   1. shoddy work; 2. a faulty car
Lend of, to have a   take advantage of a gullible person
Lezzo/Lesbo   a Lesbian
Let 'er rip   an enthusiastic start of something
Let one's hair down   behave in an informal manner
Let sleeping dogs lie   cause no further trouble
Let slip   to reveal a secret
Lick into shape   repair, fix up
Lick the dust   to die or be wounded
Licked   to be beaten or defeated
Lid   a hat
Lie doggo   1. to hide away; 2. get out of something
Lie in   stay in bed, get up late
Lie low   stay out of site
Life of Riley   a trouble free existence
Light on   horse racing short weight
Like a shag on a rock   1. a loner; 2. out of place
Like buggery   no way
Like the clappers   very fast
Line 'em up   lining up a round of drinks
Lingo   language
Lippy   lipstick
Lizard drinking, flat out like a   very busy
Loaded   1. very wealthy; 2. under the effects of alcohol or drugs, stoned
Lob/Lob in   1. arrive unannounced; 2. drop in to see someone

Lollies candy, sweets
Longneck 750ml bottle of beer in South Australia
Lucky country, the Australia
Lug 1. carry; 2. ear; 3. clumsy person
Lurk 1. underhanded racket; 2. scheme; 3. on to a good thing
Mad as a cut snake crazy, insane
Mad as a meat axe extremely mad
Mag magazine
Maggie magpie
Maidenhood virginity
Make a blue make a mistake, error
Make a quid earn a living, wage, salary
Make it snappy hurry up
Make tracks depart, leave
Make waves to cause trouble

"The Lucky Country" is a nickname used to describe Australia, taken from the 1964 book by the same name by social critic Donald Horne.

Makings, the tobacco and cigarette papers, to roll your own
Malarky foolish talk, raving on, idle gossip
Mallee unpopulated scrub or bushland
Mallee bull, fit as a very strong, fit
Man in white a cricket umpire
Man on the land a farmer or grazier
Manchester household linen
Man's best friend 1. his dog; 2. his penis
Manual a car with a manual gear shift
March down the aisle to get married
Marching orders getting the sack, to be fired
Marge margarine
Marriage on the rocks a marriage break up
Marties tomatoes
Mary's room the toilet

Mash   mashed potatoes

Mate   close friend

Mate's rate   cheaper than usual price for a friend

Matilda   a blanket roll, a swag

Metho   methylated spirits

Middy   a 10 ounce glass of beer (NSW and Western Australia)

Mike   a microphone

Milk bar   corner store that usually sells take-away food

Milko   milkman

Mince pies   the eyes

Min-min light   a strange light that appears in outback Queensland

Missus, the   a man's spouse, wife

Mite   a small child, infant

Mitt   a hand or fist

Mo   moustache

Mob   1. cattle or sheep herd; 2. group of people

Mog/Moggy   a cat

Molly dooker   a left-handed person

Money bags   a rich person

Mongrel   1. mixed-breed dog; 2. despicable person; 3. something difficult

Moniker   a person's name

Monkey suit   a dinner suit

Moo   a silly woman

Moo juice   milk

Moolah   cash, money

Moosh   mouth

Mozzie   a mosquito

Muddie   a Queensland mud crab

Mudmap   a map or a sketch drawn on the ground

Muff   female genitals

Mug 1. face; 2. one who is easily fooled; 3. friendly insult
Mulga the outback bush
Mullock spoil or rock tailings from a mine
Munga food
Murphy a potato
Mushie a mushroom
Muso a musician
Muster to herd or gather cattle or sheep
Mutt a mongrel dog
Mutton head a foolish person
My oath total agreement
Mystery bags sausages or snags

Bevan was a **muso** with **bloody** big dreams but spent most of his life **flat broke.**

Myxo myxomatosis, viral disease introduced to deplete rabbit population
NBG no bloody good
NRL National rugby league
Nab arrest, capture
Nada 1. nothing, zero, zip; 2. free
Nag 1. old inferior horse; 2. talk incessantly
Nail 1. catch, seize; 2. kill; 3. do something perfectly
Nail-biter an exciting match or game with a close finish
Nana/Narna a banana
Nanna/Nanny/Nannie grandmother
Nappy diaper
Nark a person who nags and irritates continually
Narky short-tempered
Nasho national serviceman
Natter chat, gossip
Naughty, have a have sex
Near-at-hand close by
Neato excellent, great

Neddies racing horses

Never never desert regions of Australia

New chum 1. a newcomer; 2. beginner

Newbie a newcomer to anything

Newsagent a shop where you buy newspapers, magazines and books

Nibbles a snack, small tit-bits of food

Nice drop a good wine

Nick to steal

Nick off depart, go away

Nickers women's underpants

Nigel unpopular person, has no friends

Niggly annoyed, angry

Night on the town a big night out

Nineteenth hole a bar in the golf club house

Nipper 1. a small crab or prawn; 2. a young child; 3. a young surf lifesaver

Nippy 1. cold; 2. active person

Nitwit foolish person

No drama no problem

No hoper a fool, a person without merit

No room to swing a cat a small room, cramped quarters

No worries no problem

Nob 1. annoying person; 2. head; 3. elite person

Nod off to fall asleep, have a nap

Noggin the head

Nong an idiot

Nope no

Norks breasts

North and South mouth

Nosebag meal, feed

Nosh food

Nosh up 1. very big meal; 2. to eat
Nosey parker stickybeak
Not a bad old stick a good person
Not bad good, excellent
Not for quids no way
Not much chop not good, below standards
Not on your Nellie no way
Not the full quid insane, stupid
Nothing between the ears a foolish or stupid person
Nous common sense
Nozzle the nose
Nuddy in the nude
Nugget a stocky thickset person
Nuggety a stocky thickset person, solidly built
Nulla-nulla an aboriginal club, weapon
Numb skull fool, idiot
Numbnuts ineffectual man
Numbskull dim-witted person, fool, idiot
Nut 1. head; 2. eccentric or insane person; 3. enthusiast; 4. testicle
Nut case 1. eccentric person; 2. crazy person
Nut chokers mens' underwear, briefs, underpants
Nut house an asylum
Nut out work out, solve a problem
Nutted castrated
Nympho a nymphomaniac
O.P. overproof as in rum
O.S. overseas
Oath! definitely; yes!
Obs objections
Ocean-going any seaworthy vessel

Ocker   1. stereotypical uncultured Australian; 2. destinctively Australian
Ockerism   referring to the ocker character
Odd jobs   casual work
Off colour   sick, unwell
Off like a bride's nightie   1. quickly remove clothing; 2. departed quickly
Off like a rocket   1. successful event; 2. depart quickly
Offsider   1. an assistant; 2. partner
Oi   hey you
Oinker   a pig
Okey dokey   things are good, okay
Old biddy   an old women
Old bomb   a dilapidated vehicle
Old codger   an old man
Old coot   an old person
Old fella   penis
Old flame   a lover from the past
Old fogey   an old-fashioned person
Oldies   aged parents
On a bender   drinking to excess
On a sticky wicket   in trouble
On the blink   broken down, not working
On the blower   on the phone
On the bludge   cadging money
On the cuff   on credit
On the dole   receiving social security benefits whilst unemployed
On the grog   drinking alcohol in excess
On the house   free drinks
On the level   honest
On the nose   smelly
On ya   good on you, well done

Greg spent all day **on the blower** trying to track down the **old codger** who left his **jumper** on the bus.

On your bike   get out of here, go

On your Pat Malone   on your own, alone

One and all   everybody

One and only   unique

One-arm bandit   a poker machine

One for the road   last drink

One tonner   a small truck, utility

One-eyed trouser snake   a penis

Oodles   large quantities

Op   1. surgical operation; 2. operator

Op shop   opportunity shop selling second hand goods

Optic nerve   a perve

Out cold   unconscious

Out of it   1. incapacitated as a result of alcohol or drugs; 2. spaced out

Outback   inland Australia, sparsely settled

Outstation   remote from main homestead

Over the hill   getting old

Overland trout   a goanna, lizard

Overlander   one who droves stock over long distances

Ow   sudden pain

Own up   admit, confess

Ow-ya-goin?   how are you?

Oz   Australia, an Australian

Ozzie   an Australian person

PJ's   pyjamas

Pack death   to be very afraid, scared

Pack it in   to quit

Paddo   Paddington, a suburb in Sydney and Brisbane

Paddock   an area of land enclosed by a fence

Panties   woman's underpants

The **one arm bandit** was operated by a lever on the side but today's **pokies** are operated by buttons on the front panel.

Parson's nose   the tail of a cooked chicken
Party pooper   a person who spoils a party
Pash   a kiss and cuddle
Pass away   to die
Pass round the hat   take up a collection
Pass wind   to fart
Passion pit   a drive in cinema
Pat Malone   on your own, alone
Pav   a pavlova; sweet meringue dessert cake
Payback   retaliatory action taken according to tribal code by aborigines
Pea soup   a thick fog
Pearler   something very good
Pearlies   teeth
Pecking order   social standing
Pee   urinate
Peepers   eyes
Pegs   1. legs; 2. teeth
Perve   one person lustfully eyeing another person
Petrol head   a person obsessed by his or her car
Piccaninny   an aboriginal child, baby
Picker up   a person who picks up the shorn fleeces in the sheering shed
Piddle   to urinate
Piece of piss   quite simple
Pig rooting   a horse bucking
Pig's arse   highly unlikely
Piker   one who leaves early, pulls out of a situation
Pink slip, get the   get the sack, fired; lose one's job
Pinny   an apron
Pins   legs
Pint   large glass of beer mainly in South Australia

Piss   1. to urinate; 2. alcohol
Piss head   drunkard
Piss off   depart, leave
Piss pot   an alcoholic, heavy drinker
Plate, bring a   bring a plate of food to a party or barbeque
Plates of meat   feet
Plodder   a slow worker
Plonk   very cheap wine
Pocket billiards   hands in pockets and play with genitals
Pointing Percy at the porcelain   to urinate
Pokies   poker machines
Pollies   politicians
Pommy   a British subject
Pong   a bad smell
Poofter   a homosexual man
Port   a suitcase
Postie   a mail delivery person
Pot   a ten ounce beer glass (Queensland and Victoria only)
Pozzy/Pozzie/Possie   position
Prang   a car crash, accident
Prawn   shrimp
Preggers   pregnant
Pre-loved   second-hand, used
Prezzie   a gift, present
Pubes   pubic hair
Pull your head in   mind your own business
Puffed   out of breath, tired
Pug   a boxer
Puka   large extended stomach
Puke   vomit

Aussie's love a **barbie** and a prawn on the barbie is **"the duck's guts"**.

Punch-up   a fight
Punter   a gambler; bets money on horse or dog races
Pushing up daisies   to be dead
Put down   to kill an animal
Put the hard word on   ask a favour, loan
Put the mockers on   to cause bad luck
Quack   1. a bad doctor; 2. unqualified
Quake Isles   New Zealand
Quart-pot   a billycan
Queen   a homosexual
Queer   a homosexual
Queer bird   strange person, odd
Quick as greased lightning   very quick
Quick march   hurry up
Quick quid   easy money
Quick snort   a hasty alcoholic drink
Quickie   a short sexual encounter
Quid, make a   earn a living
Quid, not the full   person with a low IQ
Quim   female genitalia
Quits   gives up easily
Quitter   to give up easily
Quoit   bum, anus
R & R   rest and recreation
RS   rat shit; feeling bad
RSL   Returned Services League
Rabbit food   green vegetables, lettuce etc.
Rabbit on   talk nonsense
Rack off   please leave
Rack up   amass

A **punch-up** followed the **barney** between Big Bruce and **queer bird Nigel**.

Radical   great, fantastic

Rafferty's rules   no rules at all

Rag   1. newspaper; 2. argue; 3. gossip; 4. handkerchief

Rage   party

Rage on   continue to party

Rager   a person who parties hard

Rain dance   a ceremony believed to cause rain

Raining cats and dogs   very heavy rain

Rank and file   general people

Rapt   overjoyed

Rare as rocking horse shit   uncommon

Rare as hen's teeth   vary rare

Rat shit   no good, bad, lousy

Ratbag   an unreliable person, fool

Ration bag   a calico bag used to carry food

Rattle the dags   get a move on, hurry up

Rattler   a railway train

Ratty   1. worn out; 2. mildly eccentric

Rave   1. big dance party; 2. type of dance music; 3. animated conversation

Raw prawn   behaved offensively

Ready to drop   very pregnant

Reckon   1. absolutely; 2. suppose

Red centre   the centre of Australia

Red Ned   cheap red wine

Red steer   a bushfire

Redback   1. a $20 note; 2. a small poisonous spider with a red back

Reefer   a marijuana cigarette

Ref   referee

Refadex   Queensland street directory

Reffo   refugee

Bert used to be **flat broke** until one day he discovered how to invest by reading the financial **rag**.

Rego   motor vehicle registration

Reject   socially unacceptable person

Rellies   relatives, relations, kin

Rep   representative

Retard   clumsy or awkward person

Rev   engine revolution

Richard Cranium   a dickhead

Ridgy-didge   1. truth, on the level; 2. original, genuine; 3. refrigerator

Right, that'd be   accepting bad news

Righty-o/Righto   yes, okay

Ringbark   to kill a tree by cutting the bark off around the trunk

Ringdinger   a two-stroke motorcycle

Ringer   1. fast sheep shearer; 2. person or thing that resembles another

Ring-in   substitute, deceive

Rip   a dangerous under-current at the beach

Rip into   begin rapidly, eagerly

Rip off   1. a poor deal, overpriced item; 2. knockoff

Rip snorter   fantastic, outstanding

Ripe   1. something gone off; 2. eager, keen; 3. drunk; 4. obscene

Ripper   great, good

Ripper, you little   exclamation of delight to good news

Rissole   1. round meat or fish patty; 2. nickname for an RSL club

Road train   a rig of two, three or four trucks drawn by a prime mover

Roadie   1. last drink; 2. drink you take when leaving a function

Rock along   travel to, go, visit

Rock on   1. come on; 2. continue

Rock up   to arrive or turn up

Rogues' gallery   police file collection of criminals' photographs

Roll a joint   roll a marijuana cigarette

Rollie   a cigarette that you roll

Rolling in it   very wealthy

Roo   a kangaroo

Roo bar   a bar fixed to a vehicle to protect it against hitting kangaroos

Root for   cheer for, encourage

Root rat   one who is always looking for sex

Rooted   1. totally exhausted; 2. broken beyond repair; 3. abuse; go away!

Ropeable   very angry

Rort   a fraud

Rotten   drunk

Rouse   lose one's temper, chastise

Rub it in   remind one of their mistakes and failures

Rubbish   1. criticise; 2. garbage, trash; 3. tease

Ruckus   a commotion

Rugrat   ankle biter, small child

Rug up   dress warmly

Run on the smell of an oily rag   a car running on very little fuel

Runabout   a small motor boat

Runs   diarrhoea

Runt   1. a small person; 2. smallest in the litter

Rush   1. strong feeling of exhilaration and pleasure; 2. very busy

Saltie   a salt water crocodile

Salvo   a member of the Salvation Army

Sammie   a sandwich

Sandgroper   a person from Western Australia

Sandshoe   jogger, sneaker, trainer

Sanga/Sanger   sandwich

Good old fashioned toasted cheese **sanga**.

Sav   a saveloy; a type of sausage

Savvy   1. understand; 2. know; 3. intelligence; 4. commonsense

Scab   1. strike breaker; 2. stingy person; 3. bludge from someone

Scallywag   mischievious person, rascal

Scalper   one who buys function tickets and then sells them at a higher price
Scaly   a crocodile
Schooner   15 ounce glass of beer (Australia wide except South Australia)
Scone   1. the head; 2. a light cake or biscuit
Scoob   a marijuana cigarette, reefer
Scorcher   a very hot day
Scrag   unattractive woman
Scratchie   instant lottery ticket
Screamer   one who gets drunk on very little alcohol
Scrounge   to borrow or collect something
Scrub   bushland
Scrub up well   1. to be well dressed; 2. look good
Scrubbers   1. wild cattle; 2. unattractive woman
See ya   goodbye, see you later
Seedy   feeling sick; especially after a drinking spree
Semi   a large truck
Send her down Huey   send down the rain
Servo   a service station
Shack   a simple house
Shades   sunglasses
Shag on a rock, stands out like a   very obvious
Shaggy dog story   a very long story or joke with a pointless ending
Shanghai   1. sling-shot; 2. involve one in an activity against their wishes
Shanty   a small bush hotel
Shark bait   a swimmer in shark infested waters
Shark biscuit   one who is new to surfing
She'll be right   everything will be okay
Sheila   a young woman
Shindig   a lively party
Shit house   1. poor quality; 2. toilet

Shonky   poor quality goods
Shoot through   leave unexpectedly
Shout   buy a round of drinks
Shove off   go away, scat
Show pony   one who is concerned with appearances
Sick   1. totally excellent, cool; 2. disgusting, revolting
Sickie   take a day off sick from work
Sicko   disgusting revolting person, depraved
Silly duffer   a silly person
Silvertail   upper crust, social climber
Singlet   tank top, vest
Siphon the python   to urinate
Skeeter   a mosquito
Skidmark   mark of faeces on underwear
Skids   brakes
Skin and blister   sister
Skin flint   miser
Skinny dipping   nude swimming
Skite   to boast or brag
Skol   drink alcohol in one gulp
Sky pilot   a clergyman, priest
Sky rocket   pocket
Slab   a 24 pack of beer
Slab hut   a bush dwelling constructed from timber slabs
Slammer   prison
Slash   to urinate
Sleepout   a porch or verandah converted to a bedroom
Slice of the cake   a share in the profits
Sling   1. a bribe; 2. tip
Slog   hard work

Bob did time in the **slammer** for **knocking off** a **one tonner** and driving it through the front window of the **milk bar**.

Sloshed   very intoxicated
Slouch hat   Australian Army hat
Sly grog   alcohol sold by an unlicensed vendor
Smoko   smoke, tea or coffee break
Snags   sausages
Snake's hiss   to urinate, piss
Snakey   bad-tempered, irritable
Snooze   sleep, doze, nap
Snorker   a sausage
Snow/Snowy   a person with white or blonde hair
Snug as a bug in a rug   cosy
So long   goodbye
Sook   a weak timid person, a cry baby
Southpaw   left-handed person
Sozzled   intoxicated
Sparky   an electrician

Aussie's love to throw a few **snags** on the **barbie.**

Sparrow fart   dawn
Spat   minor argument, fight
Specs   glasses, spectacles
Spell   to have a rest
Spew   1. to vomit; 2. very angry; 3. disappointed at something
Spewin'   very angry, upset
Spiffy   excellent, great
Spin out   1. greatly amazed; 2. a vehicle skids and spins off the road
Spit the dummy   upset
Spruiker   a person who forcefully addresses prospective customers
Sprung   caught doing wrong
Spud   a potato
Spunky   attractive sexy person
Squib   a coward

S

Squirt 1. insignificant; 2. short person; 3. little child; 4. male urination

Squizz to look

Starkers 1. totally naked; 2. insane

Station homestead, ranch

Stayer an animal (horse) or person of great endurance

Stick-up a robbery at gun point

Stickybeak a nosey person

Stirrer one who causes trouble

Stock route a track or road used by a drover

Stockman a person who looks after livestock on a large farming property

Stoked to be very happy

Stone-broke no money

Stoned drunk, intoxicated or under the influence of drugs

Stonkered 1. defeated; 2. drunk; 3. exhausted; 4. incapacitated

Storm stick umbrella

Stoush a brawl or fight

Straddie North and South Stradbroke Island; near Brisbane, Queensland

Strapped for cash short of money

Strewth 1. exclamation of surprise; 2. exclamation of irritation

Strides trousers or pants

Strine Australian slang

Stroppy in a bad temper

Stubbies men's work shorts

Stubby a small bottle of beer

Stubby cooler insulation casing for a stubby

Stuck-up haughty, conceited

Stud a male who considers himself extremely sexually attractive

Stuff 1. personal belongings; 2. render useless, ruin

Stuff it! exclamation of frustration or anger

Stuffed 1. tired; 2. worn out; 3. broken; 4. full of food

Stuffed, I'll be expression of surprise

Stunned mullet dazed

Stunner thing or person of striking beauty

Subbie a sub-contractor

Suck face French kiss

Sunbake sunbathe

Sunnies sunglasses

Sunshine State Queensland

Super 1. personal retirement fund; 2. leaded petrol; 3. very good, great

Surfie person devoted to surfing, surfboard riding

Swag a roll of blankets

Swagman/Swaggie a tramp

Swansong a last performance

Sweet tooth liking sweet foods, lollies etc

Swipe steal

Sydneysider a person who lives in Sydney

TB tuberculosis

TLC tender loving care

Ta Thank you

Tacho tachometer

Tad little bit

Taddie tadpole

Tag to follow closely

Tag along join in with others

Tail 1. buttocks; 2. follow close behind

Tail throwing pulling a beast down by the tail

Tailgate drive very close to the vehicle in front

Take a gander have a look

Take a sickie take a work sick day when you're not sick

Take a squizz have a look

The number one thing on a **surfie's** mind is catching a **bonzer** wave.

Take-away   take-out food

Take some pickies/piccies   take photographs

Tall poppie   an important, successful person

Tall poppie syndrome   to criticise important, successful people

Tallie   750ml bottle of beer

Tally   counting

Tangle foot   one who's clumsy on his feet

Tanked   intoxicated, drunk

Tarp   a tarpaulin

Tart   an immoral woman, prostitute

Tassie   Tasmania

Taswegian   a person from Tasmania

Tat   a tattoo

Tea   evening meal

Ben **tucked** into his **take-away** the minute he arrived home.

Tear into   attack physically or verbally

Tear strips off   admonish severely

Tear-arse   a wild reckless person, fast driver

Tear-jerker   something very sad

Tech   Technical college

Techie   technician

Technicolour yawn   to vomit

Tee up   to organise a meeting

Tellie   television

Territorian   a person from the Northern Territory

The axe   to be dismissed, sacked

The big A   axed; get the sack, dismissed

The big C   cancer

The big spit   to vomit

The box   television

The Cross   Kings Cross, Sydney

The Don   Sir Donald Bradman; the best ever batsman
The finger   offensive gesture made by holding up the middle finger
The missus   wife
The Rock   Uluru, Ayers Rock
The sticks   1. in the country; 2. goal posts in a game of rugby or AFL
The Territory   The Northern Territory
Thick   dopey, fool
Thick-skinned   one who does not like criticism or verbal abuse
Thin on top   going bald
Thingo   could be anything
This arvo   this afternoon
Thongs   cheap rubber backless sandals, flip-flops
Throw down   a small bottle of beer that can be drunk quickly
Thunder box   a toilet, dunny
Tick   1. credit; 2. moment or instant; 3. check mark
Ticker   the heart
Tickets on yourself   to have a high opinion of yourself
Tickle the ivories   play the piano
Tickle the Peter   to steal minor amounts from a till or cash register
Tiddly   slightly drunk, tipsy
Tide's out   beer glass needs topping up
Tie the knot   to wed
Tiff   an argument or a spat
Tiger country   rough bushland
Tight   1. unwilling to spend; 2. close; nearly even
Tight as a fish's arse   a very miserly person
Tim Tam   chocolate sandwich biscuit coated in chocolate
Tin arsed   a very lucky person
Tinned dog   canned meat, camp pie
Tinnie   1. a can of beer; 2. a small aluminium boat; 3. lucky

Tip   1. offer a racing tip to someone; 2. rubbish dump

Tipsy   slightly drunk

Tit   female breast

Tit for tat   a hat

Toey   1. nervous, apprehensive; 2. keen, ready to go

Togs   a bathing suit, clothes

Tomahawk   a small axe

Too right   definitely

Top drop   a good bottle of wine or a good beer

Top end   northern part of the Northern Territory

Tosser   annoying person, jerk

Trackie daks   tracksuit pants

Trackies   track suit

Troppo   gone mad, insane

Trots   1. having diarrhoea; 2. harness horse racing

Truckie   a truck driver

True blue   1. genuine; 2. a loyal person

Tuck in   to eat, have a meal

Tucker   food

Tucker bag   a food carrying bag

Turps   1. alcoholic drink; 2. turpentine

Turps, hit the   a drinking binge

Tweeds   trousers, pants

The **trots** is a horse race focusing on the horse's gait and requires the horse to pull a two-wheeled cart called a sulky.

Twinkle toes   a good dancer

Twit   a dull, stupid person

Two-pot screamer   a very cheap drunk

Two-up   a gambling game with two coins, heads or tails

Tyke   a Roman Catholic

U-ee   a U turn on the road

Ugg boots/Uggies   boots made of sheepskin

Ugly as sin a very ugly person
Umpie umpire
Umpteen many, large amount
Unco awkward, clumsy person
Under the weather 1. feeling poorly; 2. hungover
Underdaks underpants
Underdog a team or organisation not expected to win
Undies underpants
Uni university
Unit a flat or apartment
Unreal! excellent!
Unsung hero a person who is not celebrated or recognised
Unwind to relax, take it easy
Up a gum tree in difficulties
Up and about active after an illness or sleep
Up at sparrow fart rising very early
Up oneself have a high opinion of oneself
Up somebody, to get to berate somebody
Up the creek in a barbed wire canoe without a paddle bad situation
Up the duff pregnant
Up to putty no good, worthless
Urger a racecourse tipster
Useful as tits on a bull 1. incompetent person; 2. useless person or thing
User 1. one who exploits other people; 2. drug addict
Ute a utility; open-backed work vehicle
VB Victoria bitter, a popular Australian beer
Vacuum a vacuum cleaner
Valley, the Fortitude Valley, Brisbane
Vamoose depart quickly
Vee-dub a Volkswagen car

Veg out   relax
Vegemite   a dark-brown savoury sandwich spread made from yeast extract
Veggies   vegetables
Vego   a vegetarian
Verbal diarrhoea   constant talking
Vet   1. Veterinary surgeon; 2. a war veteran
Vibe   1. atmosphere; 2. feeling; 3. rhythm; 4. signals sent out to someone
Vinnie's   St Vincent de Paul charity shop
Vino   wine
Vocal   vocabulary
WACA   1. Western Australian Cricket Association; 2. Perth cricket ground
Wacked   1. exhausted; 2. out of it
Waddie   a baton or club
Wadjamacallit   something you don't know the name of
Waffle   talking nonsense
Wag   1. an amusing person, a joker; 2. skip school, truancy
Walkabout   1. gone missing; 2. an extended trip or tour on foot
Wallop   thrash, punch with force
Walloper   a policeman
Wally   1. a stupid person; 2. wallet
Waltzing Matilda   1. carry one's swag; 2. well known Australian song
Wanker   1. a stupid person; 2. an arrogant person; 3. an amusing person
Wanna   want to
Wanna-be   one who tries very hard without success
Washer   a face towel
Wasted   1. exhausted; 2. under the effects of alcohol or drugs
Water bag   a portable water container
Water the horse   to urinate
Watering hole   one's favourite pub or hotel
Way   extremely

Weaner   a calf no longer feeding from its mother

Wedding tackle   a male's sexual organs

Wedgie   prank where one's pants are grabbed and pulled up sharply

Wee   urine, to urinate

Weekend warrior   person in the army reserve

Weekender   holiday house

Weenies   small frankfurts

Well-heeled   a wealthy person

Well-to-do   rich, prosperous

Wellies   Wellington boots or gumboots

Wet, the   rainy season in Northern Australia from December to March

Wettie   a wetsuit

Whacked   drunk, intoxicated

Whaler   a bush nomad

Wharfie   a dock worker

What's the damage?   how much does it cost?

Whatsaname   used when unable to recall real name of person or thing

When the eagle shits   pay day

Whew   expressing relief

Whiffie   offensive smell

Whinge   to whimper, complain

Whip around   collect money

Whipped   defeated

White pointers   topless female sunbathers or bathers

Whirlybird   a helicopter

White ant   to go behind someone's back

White leghorn   a female lawn bowler

Whoop whoop   a long way away

Whose shout?   whose turn to buy the drinks?

Wifey   your wife or spouse

Wig warmer   a hat

Willie   a penis

Willy willy   a brief dust storm of cyclonic nature

Wimp   a weak person

Windies   West Indian cricket team

Wing-ding   a big party

Wino   alcoholic, addicted to wine

Winkers   the eyes

Witchety grub   a large white grub found in wood

Wizz   to urinate

Wobbly   losing your temper

Wog   1. flu or a cold; 2. annoying insect; 3. person of Mediterranean origin

Wombat   one who eats, roots and leaves

Wonky   1. unstable, unsteady; 2. poor condition

Wooden spoon   a prize for coming last

Woofer   a dog

Woofter   a homosexual man

Woolshed   a shed where sheep are shorn

Woop woop   1. middle of nowhere; 2. small insignificant town

Wouldn't be dead for quids   to be alive and well

Wouldn't piss on you if you were on fire   expression of utter contempt

Wouldn't work in an iron lung   a very lazy person

Wowser   1. a non drinker; 2. a puritan

Wrung-out   exhausted, tired-out

Wuss   timid person, coward

XXXX   Queensland Four X Beer

Ya   you, your

Yabber   talk a lot, chat

Yabbie/Yabby   Australian freshwater crayfish

Yack   1. talk a lot; 2. chat; 3. vomit

The freshwater **yabby** is often caught for food.

Yachtie   a person who sails on yachts
Yacker/Yakka/Yakker   hard work
Yahoo   1. a reckless person, lout, uncouth; 2. exclamation of delight
Yair/Yeah   yes
Yank   1. an American; 2. to tell a lie
Yank tank   large American manufactured car
Yap   talk continuously
Yarn   1. a story; 2. talking with somebody
Yikes   mild exclamation of concern
Yobbo   a rude person, lout, hooligan
Yodel   to vomit
Yonks   a long period of time
You beaut/beauty   something good
You wish   an expression referring to one with unrealistic expectations
Young'un   a youngster
You're not wrong   you are right
Youse   plural for you
Yowie   mythical monster
Yuck   expression of disgust, unpleasant
Yuppie   young urban professional person with a high disposable income
Z grade   the lowest quality
Zac/Zack   old currency (sixpence) now five cents
Zap   1. cook in the microwave; 2. annihilate; 3. electric shock; 4. exhausted
Zebra crossing   a pedestrian crossing with broad white painted lines
Zeds   sleep, snooze
Ziff   unshaven, beard
Zilch   nil, nothing
Zip   zero, nothing
Zit   acne, pimples
Zonked   1. very tired; 2. drunk

Notes